MW00764491

God Listens
When You're Afraid

PRAYERS FOR WHEN ANIMALS SCARE YOU

CAROL J. ADAMS

THE PILGRIM PRESS   CLEVELAND

For

SUSAN ALLISON,

who taught me

The Pilgrim Press, 700 Prospect Avenue, Cleveland, Ohio 44115-1100
thepilgrimpress.com
Copyright © 2006 Carol J. Adams

Printed in the United States of America on acid-free paper

10   09   08   07   06   5   4   3   2   1

Library of Congress Cataloging-in-Publication Data

Adams, Carol J.
    God listens when you're afraid : prayers for when animals scare you /
Carol J. Adams.
        p. cm.   (God listens)
        ISBN-13: 978-0-8298-1741-6 (alk. paper)
        1. Prayers for animals—Juvenile literature.   2. Fear in children.   3. Fear—
Juvenile literature.   I. Title.   II. Series: Adams, Carol J. God listens.
BV283.A63A323—2006
242'.82—dc22

                                                            2006012489

ISBN-13 : 978-0-8298-1741-6
ISBN-10 : 0-8298-1741-7

Contents

Contents

Dear Friend,

It's no fun to be scared, is it? But you are not the only one who is afraid of animals. Many people—including grown-ups—were afraid of animals when they were younger; some still are. Many of your friends probably share your fears, but they may be too ashamed to talk about it.

People respond to their fears in many different ways. That is what is different—not the fear, but the way people respond.

Being afraid of animals is an experience you share with many others. Talking about being afraid—that is not as common.

Lots of things keep us from talking about it. You might feel ashamed. You might feel no one will understand. But you know what? Fears that are kept quiet, fears that we keep locked inside, often grow. They gobble us up if no one challenges them. But fears that are shared, that are brought into the light, often shrink.

By talking about being scared you begin to look at your fear and understand how it works. So it is good to ask for help. You can say, "I feel scared of _____. Can you help me?"

Perhaps you have already told someone about being afraid. Perhaps you trusted someone and it didn't help;

perhaps that person laughed at you or in other ways failed to listen to your fears. I am sorry that happened. But there are others who will understand you, and there is One who can hear all your secret fears.

You can tell God about your feelings, about what scares you, about how being scared makes you feel—sad, or angry, or lonely, or confused. Because these feelings are quite powerful, it is good to share them with God. God will listen to your concerns about yourself and about the animals who scare you. You can ask God for help.

In some of the prayers in this book I have left a blank space for you to fill in the name of the animal who scares you. If there is any prayer that is not about the animal who scares you but speaks about your feelings, just substitute the animal who scares you for the animal in the prayer.

If there is a prayer about an animal who has scared you that you wish would be written, please let me know. You can write me care of The Pilgrim Press, 700 Prospect Avenue, Cleveland, OH 44115-1100, or by e-mail to cja@caroljadams.com.

Dear friend, you are not alone. God listens when you're afraid.

I wish I could like animals,

    but they scare me.

They drool on me.

They make noises I am not used to.

They move too fast; they jump on me.

They do strange things.

They act in ways I cannot predict.

People say they aren't scary, that they can't hurt me.

But I see many ways they can hurt me.

What would I do?

I am afraid that I don't know what to do.

If I run away, they'll chase me;

If I stand still, they'll bite me.

I don't know what I could to do to stop them.

I don't know how to stay safe.

I am very worried.

God, there is so much I love about your world.

Trees invite me to lean on them,

lawns to sit upon them,

hills to run down them.

But, God, in my leaning,

in my sitting, in my running

I see bugs climbing, crawling, flying.

They scare me.

I don't know when they will be climbing toward me,

crawling upon me,

flying into me.

God, how can I be fair to all that exists in your world?

How do I balance what I love and what I fear?

Please help me.

That animal just now, he scared me.

He would not stop coming toward me.

I said stop!

He didn't listen.

I screamed!

I ran the other way.

He followed.

I cried.

Why didn't anyone help me?

Hold me, God.

Let me cry.

It was so scary.

Dear God,

When I am scared I forget how to breathe.

My heart races like a horse.

My stomach muscles get so tight

 I think they will never get unstuck.

It feels like my skin is on inside out.

My hands are all sweaty.

My shoulders and neck feel tense,

 and I have a headache.

My hair is standing on end

 and I feel goose bumps all over.

All I can think about is what scares me.

I can't think of anything else.

It's like I'm in a tunnel and there is nothing else to see.

I can't run away.

I can't move.

I don't like feeling scared.

I want to feel brave, like a superhero.

Why can't I be like a superhero and fight?

Then I would know what it feels like not to be scared.

God, if I can't be a superhero,

Can you help me be safe?

Dear God,

I'm afraid of _____ .

I don't know how to explain this.

I don't know what to say.

I can't find any words to help me.

Why can't my heart beating so fast

    speak for itself?

Why do I have to explain it?

I'm not being stubborn.

I'm scared.

I can't get to sleep.

My stomach's upset.

I'm afraid.

I need people in my life to say,

   "You don't have to say anything.

    It's okay to be scared."

In my room, there are things I fear.

I once saw a spider in the corner of my ceiling.

In the summer, by the window,

    I heard a mosquito buzzing.

At night, the light casts strange shadows.

The house creaks.

Something lives in the closet.

I saw something move under my bed.

I'm afraid to go to sleep.

If I shut my eyes it might come out of the closet.

If I get out of bed, I'm afraid it might grab my legs.

Somebody told me that if I laughed at it

    Whatever I feared would get smaller

    and then disappear.

Help me laugh, God.

Dear God,

Bugs inside the house scare me.

Bugs don't belong inside the house.

Bugs belong outside.

Geckos inside the house scare me

Geckos don't belong here.

They are out of place here.

Mice inside the house scare me.

Mice shouldn't come inside.

If I could see them from far away

Maybe they wouldn't be scary.

But they aren't far away.

They're in the house:

That is the problem.

Why did my mother scream

    when she saw the mouse

    run across the floor?

Did she scream because he moved so quickly

    across the floor?

Or because his tail was so long?

I didn't know my parents were afraid of anything.

What am I going to do?

I'm not a grown-up.

God, can you help me?

Just because someone else is afraid,

I don't have to be, do I?

Dear God,

I'm afraid of holes.

I'm afraid of holes and what lives in them.

It's dark inside a hole.

What if I fall down?

What if my foot stumbles on a hole and gets stuck?

If I see a hole, I avoid it,

but sometimes a hole is hidden

and what lives in it comes out.

Help me to see that those holes

are homes for _____ ,

that the hole is like a nest,

or an apartment or a house.

I'm not afraid of my home;

God, can you help me

not to be afraid of their homes?

God, I love to play where there is a swing set,

   a sandbox, a picnic table.

But then I hear a noise.

A bug flies by and lands on my arm

Sometimes it's a dragonfly;

   to me it looks ferocious.

Sometimes it's a ladybug. People say it's lucky,

But I'm scared when they come near me.

I itch all over just thinking about them.

When I see bugs on the ground

I want to step on them.

They are invading my world, aren't they?

Or am I invading their world?

Help me understand that not all bugs sting.

Help me understand that

   they may look fierce to protect their nests.

Would I do the same thing?

Dear God,

I'd like to be able to tell you why I don't like snakes.

I'd like to be able to say it is because they don't have

any legs.

Or because of the way they slither.

Or because they can move so fast—

sometimes they dart out of the grass

and then disappear.

But the big ones can move so slowly

and they are wider than my leg.

It's not that I feel small;

in fact, sometimes I tower over them.

But, all the same, they scare me!

They have the power to hurt me.

Not just the poisonous ones,

but the poisonous ones, of course.

It is hard for me to see that

I might have disturbed their home,

Or scared them and that is why they are moving so fast.

My heart beats so fast when I see one!

Can you help me slow my heart down?

How can I feel safe when they are around?

How can I feel safe when I don't know

    whether they are around or not?

Can you help me see them as one of your creatures?

Because right now, God, they are very scary.

I don't want to think about rats, God.

If I tell myself, "It's all right,

　　you don't have to think about them,"

do you think I can get my brain

　　to stop thinking about how they scurry?

Or how long their tails are?

It makes me shiver.

Then I can't get them out of mind.

They scurry through my thoughts.

How do I stop thinking about them?

Slow my thoughts down, please, God.

Help me take a deep breath.

Help me fill my mind with something good,

　　Something happy.

Dear God,

Bats are scary the way they fly and dart.

I am afraid one is going to fly into my hair.

Then what would I do?

The bat would get caught there.

I could get bitten.

When I see a bat fly by,

    that is all that I can think about.

Someone said if I learned about bats

then maybe they wouldn't scare me.

Someone said if I can see they have a purpose,

    then I could see them differently.

They have a built-in radar,

    so actually they can avoid things in their way, like me.

They eat insects,

    so the insects won't bite me.

Thank you, bato.

Small beings scare me.

They move fast.

You can barely see them,

    and then they're gone.

God, why do grown-ups ask me

    "Oh, you're not scared of that small thing, are you?"

Yes, I am.

Why do they make me feel bad?

I am not being silly.

Why can't they see that

    small is what makes them scary?

Why does being the giant in the world of the small

    not give me comfort?

I know being scared doesn't make any sense

    to anyone else.

I know I'm bigger than they are.

I know they have more to be afraid of than I do.

So why am I still scared?

Some people say small is beautiful,

God, help me see that.

But also help the grown-ups

to see that my fears are real.

Dear God,

When I walk down the street

and see a dog on a leash,

I hope the person holds tight.

When I visit friends and they have a dog,

I hope I don't ever have to see the dog.

Dogs scare me.

I don't like when they jump on me or lick me.

They smell.

They bark and growl.

Their paws are dirty.

Their hair sticks to my clothes.

Even the dogs that people say are friendly frighten me.

How do I know a dog won't bite me?

No one understands why I am afraid of dogs.

They say, "Dogs are so nice and friendly."

I don't believe them!

They want me to get near dogs.

I don't want to be near dogs.

No matter what they say,

I am not on a first-name basis with dogs.

They say, "Just pat her head, you'll see."

I don't want to pat her head.

Why won't they understand?

I hate it when I'm told I'm wrong to be afraid,

that all I have to do is come forward,

come near.

I say they aren't listening.

Dear God, I feel mad.

Come near and comfort me, God.

Why does my neighbor's dog hate me?

Why does that dog

    charge into the fence when I am walking near?

I know he is growling and barking at me.

One day the neighbors left their gate open

    and I knew their dog would come out and get me.

The dog doesn't know me.

My parents say the dog is just doing his job,

    protecting the house.

The dog doesn't know that I am a nice person.

My dog is not that big.

My dog is not as big as the one who lives down the street.

Tonight my cat came home and was bleeding.

I worry about the rabbits.

How can I protect them?

How can I keep them safe?

Can my prayers protect them?

Will you protect them?

Watch over my animal friends, please, God.

Dear God,

I love Garfield,

   but I am afraid of cats.

Heathcliff is funny,

   but I am still afraid of cats.

God, why did you make me

   so that I am afraid of cats?

If it were snakes, people would understand.

Or mice. Lots of kids are afraid of them.

But cats?

Cats purr.

Cats come up to you and meow.

But cats snarl!

Cats scratch.

Cats attack birds and small animals.

I don't see them as being sweet and cuddly.

28

I think of their claws.

I think of their teeth.

Don't other people see this about cats?

They say, "It's only a cat!"

I want to shout! "What do you know?"

They don't know me

and they don't know cats.

Is there something more

I could learn about cats to help me?

Are there any cats like

Garfield and Heathcliff I could meet?

Dear God,

Today I was walking home

and saw a dead animal by the side of the road

and there were all these bugs flying around,

and I couldn't get that picture out of my head.

Now I'm trying to go to bed

    and it's all I can think about.

I remember the time I saw _____ .

That scared me the most of all.

How do the thoughts get stopped?

It's like a movie going on and on in my head.

How can I stop the movie?

In my head, can I change the channel?

Could I go and get popcorn?

Can I turn it off?

I wonder how the animal died.

I feel sorry for the animal.

Was the animal somebody's pet?

Is he or she wondering what happened

    to that special friend?

Is an animal family missing a mother or a father?

Dear God, please keep animals safe—

they need your care and so do I.

God, I had the flu last year.

I remember staying home from school

And going to the doctor to get help.

The flu is no fun, even though I got special food.

The doctor says each flu is different.

Bird flu is the worst yet . . .

The newspapers say people die from it.

Can I catch it? If I touch a bird, will I get sick?

Now I'm scared when I see birds.

I saw pigeons on the ground and

    wanted to throw rocks at them to

    get them to fly away.

Bird flu is scary. Farmers are killing so many birds

    to prevent the flu spreading to us.

Help me God,

help me to know what can be done,

    for me and for the birds.

God, forests look so beautiful.

I love all the trees.

But trees make it dark in a forest

and that scares me.

Then I hear sounds in the forest.

And I think: What is coming near?

Is it going to hurt me?

Is it is a bear? Or a wolf?

A skunk? Or a porcupine?

Does it like the dark?

Is it hiding from me?

Help me, God. I love trees.

It's your animals who scare me.

Dear God,

Let me list what is wrong with visiting a farm.

Frogs, for one.

Frogs move in and out of water.

Why can't they decide

    where they want to be and stay there?

I don't trust them.

Chickens look so different.

Ducks and geese

    with their big beaks that move so fast,

    ducks and geese that chase you,

    and that are so loud.

Roosters too.

Horses are too big, and cows seem noisy.

What are they doing?

What are they saying?

I feel like a stranger to them.

They scare me.

Help me see the farm as a community,

a neighborhood,

where all the neighbors are different.

And I am too.

Dear God,

I looked out at the water

    and thought I saw a fin.

How can I go into the water?

There is something waiting for me there,

    something I can't see.

I'm afraid of sharks,

    but I love porpoises.

I'm afraid of jellyfish,

    but I love to see the crabs walking sideways.

I'm scared when I walk in the water:

I can't see my feet.

It feels funny.

Fish come too close to me,

    and the seaweed scares me.

Everything is different.

They don't breathe air.

It's like going into someone else's world.

I don't belong here.

They don't want me here.

God, I'd like to feel welcome here.

Dear God,

Are the dinosaurs really dead?

What if they are hiding somewhere,

    waiting to come back?

Those meat eaters were very quick and very deadly.

I can't stop thinking about their teeth and claws,

    about how powerful they were.

I feel small and helpless.

I know they could kill me.

God, I don't like thinking these thoughts.

But once I start I don't know how to stop.

Can you help me, God?

Help me know that I am safe,

That I am safe, right now,

And that the dinosaurs are gone forever.

Dear God,

When I saw _____,

something happened.

My body sent a message to every part of me:

Watch out! Danger is here! Pay attention!

That is why my heart is beating so fast.

And I can't find any words.

I am watching out.

I am paying attention.

It's a good thing to watch out.

My heart is pumping blood.

It gives me energy.

If I had to, I could run away.

But I don't have to.

I want these feelings to go away.

My fear was trying to protect me,

But now I can't stop.

Dear God,

My body is very important to me.

It's mine.

No one should be able to touch it

without my permission.

And that means animals, too.

I do not want to be licked

just because a dog or cat wants to.

I do not want to be jumped on.

I do not want bugs landing on me

or crawling on me

I don't want anyone to bite me.

I do not like thinking about it—

Being licked.

Being jumped on.

Being crawled on.

Why is this called fear?

It makes sense to me.

I've been told animals have

    more reasons to be scared of us

    than we do of them.

Can there be a place where animals

and people are friendly to each other?

If I promise not to hurt them,

Will they promise not to hurt me?

Dear God,

Why is my brother afraid of spiders?

I don't like snakes, but spiders don't scare me.

You made us all so very different from each other

And yet we are also so very much alike.

We like different kinds of candy.

We have different favorite superheroes.

Sometimes we have different fears.

How can I help my brother?

"I'm not scared . . . I'm not scared . . ."

If I say it enough, will it be true?

"I'm not scared."

"I'm not scared."

It doesn't seem to be working.

I am still frightened when I think of _____.

God, can I change the way I feel?

Can you help me change the way I feel?

Dear God,

I was told that if I know how to feel safe

I don't have to be afraid.

If I could stay in my bed,

    then maybe I'd feel safe.

If I could stay near to my parents,

    then maybe I'd feel safe.

But is there a way for me to feel safe

    when I'm all alone?

But I'm not alone, am I?

God, you are with me.

Help me to feel your protective presence.

It's okay, I tell myself.

Everything will be all right.

No one is going to hurt me.

Take a deep breath.

It's okay.

Think of something that makes me happy.

Take another deep breath.

It's okay.

I can handle this.

I'll stand on my tiptoes and stretch.

I'll look at a cloud.

It's okay, I tell myself.

I can handle this.

God, can you help make this true?

God, how can I love what you created?

You created some very scary animals.

Animals with sharp teeth and claws

    who could hurt me.

Not just furry mammals,

But also reptiles, with wrinkled, furless skin.

And bugs, crawling, flying, biting, stinging bugs.

I know there was a reason you created them.

I just don't know why you did.

Why did you create all these dangerous beings?

Help me understand the purpose

    each of them has in the world.

Help me see how we are connected.

A NOTE TO FAMILY AND FRIENDS

Do you remember something that scared you when you were young? Every adult I have talked to remembers an animal—or many—whom they feared. Remembering your own fear can be one of the most helpful things in reaching out to your child.

The most important action you can take is to listen to your children's feelings. Don't criticize their fears or pretend they don't exist. Don't say, "There's nothing to worry about." Do say, "That felt scary, didn't it?" Help them name their feelings. Ask them, "What were you worried would happen?" Reassure them, "You are safe." Tell them something that worried you. Let them know that everyone is afraid of something and that fears are a normal part of growing up. Help them feel more confident. Provide positive ways to respond to fear. Go to the library and ask your children's librarian for some books about being afraid. Read the prayers in this book together. Let your child know you are saying a prayer for him or her.

A PRAYER FOR MY CHILD

God, I pray right now for my child, _____ .

Please be present to _____ as she/he prays to You.

You know I would gladly take on the pain

and fear of my child—if only I could.

It hurts so deeply to see _____ suffer.

What can I do?

God, I remember when I was little

I was so afraid of _____ .

I still am—but not the same as then.

Now I fear _____ more.

God, help me talk with my child.

Please help her/him know your comfort

when she/he feels alone and scared.

Please provide your healing presence here.

Please remind each of us, God, that we are not alone.